EXCAVATING THE PAST

ANCIENT EGYPT

Jackie Gaff

Heinemann Library
Chicago, Illinois

Designed by Carole Binding
Originated by Ambassador Litho Ltd
Printed in China by WKT Company Limited

09 08 07 06 05
10 9 8 7 6 5 4 3 2

**Library of Congress Cataloging-
in-Publication Data**
A copy of the cataloging-in-publication data
for this title is on file with the Library of
Congress.
    Ancient Egypt / Jackie Gaff.
    ISBN 1-4034-4836-1 (HC), 1-4034-5456-6
    (Pbk.)

Acknowledgments
The author and publisher are grateful to
the following for permission to reproduce
photographs: pp. 5, 15 bottom, 21 top, 21
bottom, 22, 23, 33 bottom Bridgeman Art Library;
pp. 6, 8, 9 top, 9 bottom, 10, 11 top, 12, 14 top,
14 bottom, 16, 18 top, 19 bottom, 24, 25 top,
25 bottom, 26, 27, 28 left, 28 right, 29 top, 29
bottom, 30, 32, 33 top, 33 right, 34 top, 34
bottom, 35 top, 35 bottom, 36, 38 left, 39, 40, 41
top, 41 bottom Art Archive; p. 7 Hulton-Deutsch
Collection/Corbis; pp. 13, 19 top, 38 right Werner
Forman; p. 15 top Alexander Tsiaras/Science Photo
Library; p. 43 Philippe Plailly, Eurelios/Science
Photo Library.

Cover photograph of the Great Sphinx
and the Great Pyramid at Giza reproduced
with permission of Digital Stock. Small
photograph of the death mask that covered
Tutankhamen's mummy reproduced with
permission of Werner Forman Archive.

The publisher would like to thank Richard
Parkinson, of the British Museum (London),
and Emily Teeter, of the Oriental Institute
(Chicago), for their help in the preparation
of this book.

Every effort has been made to contact
copyright holders of any material reproduced
in this book. Any omissions will be rectified
in subsequent printings if notice is given to
the publisher.

Some words are shown in bold, **like this**.
You can find out what they mean by
looking in the glossary.

CONTENTS

THE ANCIENT EGYPTIAN WORLD

Nearly 5,000 years have passed since the ancient Egyptians began creating one of the world's earliest, greatest, and longest-lasting civilizations. In their lands beside the Nile River, they founded magnificent cities where all kinds of knowledge flourished, from **astronomy** and **engineering** to mathematics and medicine. The most awe-inspiring Egyptian achievements were in art and architecture. They carved amazing sculptures and decorated walls with fabulous paintings. They built vast **temples,** and gigantic stone pyramids as **tombs** for their rulers, the **pharaohs.**

Out with the old

The civilization flourished for nearly 3,000 years, but eventually Egypt was weakened by **civil war** and invasion by foreign powers. In 332 B.C.E., Egypt was invaded by the Greeks, led by Alexander the Great, and became part of his empire. About 300 years later Egypt was conquered by the Romans. In the following centuries, Christianity was introduced to Egypt, and churches and monasteries replaced the ancient temples as centers of worship. In the 600s, Egypt was invaded by Arab peoples and became the mainly Muslim country it is today.

△ *The Egyptian civilization would not have developed without the Nile River. The fertile land beside it could be farmed, whereas the regions to the west and east were barren desert. The Nile provided fish and other animals to eat, and mud for making pots and building houses. It was also Egypt's main highway, with people traveling the length of the country by boat.*

Lost in the mists of time

The ancient Egyptian language and way of life were slowly lost. Many buildings were destroyed or buried beneath rubble and sand, but larger stone structures, such as the great temples and pyramids, survived. Egypt became popular with foreign tourists from ancient Greek and Roman times onward. Although travelers wondered at the ancient stone monuments, no one knew what they were. **Medieval** European **pilgrims**, for instance, remembered the Bible story about Joseph storing grain during Egypt's seven years of **famine** and thought that the pyramids were his granaries.

In with the new

Proper scientific study of the ancient remains only began in 1798, when the French emperor Napoleon and his army invaded Egypt. The French were defeated by the British and forced to leave Egypt in 1801. However, a team of artists and scientists had traveled with Napoleon's army to record all they could discover about Egypt, ancient and modern. The team carried out the first detailed **survey** of ancient Egyptian monuments and laid the foundations of **Egyptology**—the study of the language, culture, and history of ancient Egypt.

▽ *This engraving is from a book by Domenique Vivant Denon about Napoleon's expedition to Egypt in 1798. It shows French scientists measuring the Great **Sphinx** at Giza.*

DID YOU KNOW? Ancient Greek and Roman tourists carved graffiti on ancient Egyptian monuments.

The development of archaeology

Hunting for treasure

The findings of Napoleon's artists started a worldwide fashion for collecting ancient **artifacts** (called **antiquities** at that time). So, collectors flocked to Egypt in the early 1800s. Unfortunately, most collectors were only interested in discovering unusual or valuable antiquities such as gold jewelry, and they did not care how much damage they did in the process. Battering rams and even explosives were used to open up sites, and so countless everyday objects were lost forever, along with a wealth of information. Other sites were robbed by local people, for antiquities they could sell to foreigners.

◁ *Many antiquities were taken out of Egypt in the early 1800s, and some of them formed the basis of the great collections now held in museums around the world. This painting shows a statue of the pharaoh Rameses II being taken from Luxor for a dealer named Giovanni Belzoni. The statue is now in the British Museum, London, England.*

Rescue operation

The plundering situation was saved largely by Frenchman Auguste Mariette (1821–1881), who arrived in Egypt in 1850. Mariette was determined to stop the looting and destruction of antiquities, and to make sure that finds were properly studied and cared for. In 1858, the Egyptian ruler Said Pasha made Mariette director of the new Egyptian Antiquities Service. It was Mariette's responsibility to supervise all **excavations** in Egypt and to police the **export** of antiquities. He was also given permission to set up Egypt's first museum of antiquities, the Egyptian Museum in Cairo.

WHO WAS Sir William Flinders Petrie?

*Sir William Flinders Petrie was one of the first scientific excavators in the history of Egyptian archaeology, establishing techniques that are still used today. He was born in England in 1853 and traveled to Egypt in the early 1880s. By the time he left in 1923, he had led excavations at almost every major site in the country. He continued working on **digs** until shortly before he died, at the age of 89, in 1942.*

Pioneering practice

The late 1800s saw the development of true **archaeology**—the scientific excavation and study of the remains of past civilizations. In Egypt, its pioneers included Sir William Flinders Petrie (1853–1942) from England and George Reisner (1867–1942) from the United States. Both men understood the value of careful excavation, and of recording everything they found. They knew that everything discovered, from pottery and bones to artwork and buildings, could provide clues about how people once lived and died. It is thanks to the practice of scientific archaeology that so much evidence has survived to tell us the story of everyday life in ancient Egyptian times.

Archaeology Challenge

Petrie invented a way of dating and classifying objects by their appearance, which is known as sequence dating. Through studying **prehistoric** pots, he realized that their shapes and patterns differed over time and could give useful clues about when they were made. Although modern techniques for dating objects, such as **radiocarbon dating**, are more exact, sequence dating is still used to give a rough date to objects found on digs.

UNLOCKING THE LANGUAGE

Written evidence is incredibly important in helping archaeologists find out about the past. The ancient Egyptians were among the first people to use writing. A range of written records—from legal documents to letters and poems—have helped us to piece their story together. But, at first, archaeologists had a problem: no one knew how to read Egyptian writing!

▽ *This example of ancient Egyptian writing on* **papyrus** *dates from the 1st century* B.C.E.

Archaeology Challenge

Epigraphy is a branch of **archaeology** concerned with recording **inscriptions** such as writings, carvings, and paintings. The first official epigraphers began work in Egypt in the 1890s and, although equipment has improved over the years, the techniques have remained much the same. A photograph is taken. Then the photographed inscription is traced in ink. Finally, the tracing is compared with the original to check that the record is accurate.

Lost languages

Instead of an alphabet, the Egyptians wrote with picture symbols called **hieroglyphs**. Most of the symbols stood for sounds, but some stood for ideas. Two other scripts evolved from hieroglyphs, **hieratic** and **demotic**. In about the 1st century B.C.E., the **Coptic** script developed. Coptic was written with the 24 letters of the Greek alphabet and 6 signs taken from demotic. Coptic slowly replaced the other three scripts, and within a few hundred years there was no one left who could understand them.

▷ *An oval frame with the names of an Egyptian ruler written inside in hieroglyphs is called a cartouche. The term comes from the French word for an oval-shaped gun cartridge. It was first used by the scholars who accompanied Napoleon's 1798 invasion of Egypt.*

The Rosetta Stone

The key to translating ancient Egyptian writing was found at Rosetta in 1799 by a soldier in Napoleon's army. The Rosetta Stone is a large slab of polished granite, dating from the 2nd century B.C.E. It has the same text carved into it in three languages—hieroglyphic, demotic, and Greek, the language spoken by Egypt's ruling classes after the country was absorbed into the Greek Empire. It is thought to have been carved in 196 B.C.E. Copies were made of the carvings and studied by scholars who understood ancient Greek. Some of them realized that the royal names they could read in the Greek text were the words in **cartouches** in the hieroglyphic text. Others used their knowledge of Coptic to work out what some of the demotic signs stood for. Finally, in 1822, Jean-François Champollion cracked the code of the Rosetta Stone, becoming the first person since ancient times to understand the meaning of Egyptian hieroglyphs.

WHO WAS Jean-François Champollion?

Born in France in 1790, Champollion became passionate about languages at school, studying Latin, Greek, Arabic, Coptic, and other ancient languages. He published his first book on Egypt when he was 21 and solved the mystery of the hieroglyphs in 1822, when he was 32. He visited Egypt only once, in 1828–1829. He died after a stroke in 1832.

▷ *After the British defeated Napoleon's army in 1801, the Rosetta Stone was taken to the British Museum in London, where it still is today.*

DID YOU KNOW? Writing was invented nearly 6,000 years ago by the Mesopotamians.

Egyptian scribes and scholars

Most of the written evidence we have from ancient Egyptian times was created by educated men called **scribes**. All the top jobs in the government, army, and priesthood were held by scribes. Most other scribes worked as ordinary civil servants, doing everything from collecting taxes to recording law cases. Others became scholars or artists, or worked as teachers or librarians.

Being a good scribe was a passport to success, but only wealthy families could afford to educate their children. Ordinary children did not go to school. Instead, their fathers taught them a trade. Education was only for boys. A few girls may have learned to read and write, but most stayed at home and were taught household skills by their mothers.

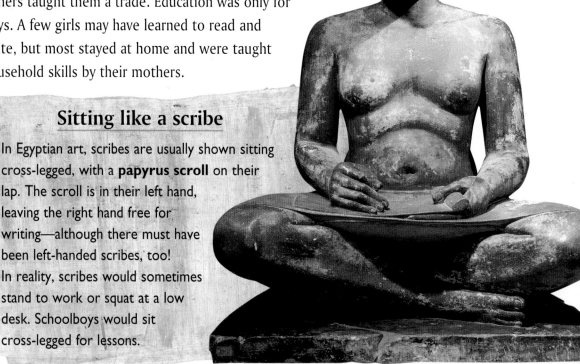

EYEWITNESS

"Be a scribe! It saves you from labor and protects you from all kinds of work. It spares you from using the hoe and the mattock [from farming] . . . It saves you from having to row a boat . . ."

(Ancient Egyptian advice to a schoolboy)

Sitting like a scribe

In Egyptian art, scribes are usually shown sitting cross-legged, with a **papyrus scroll** on their lap. The scroll is in their left hand, leaving the right hand free for writing—although there must have been left-handed scribes, too! In reality, scribes would sometimes stand to work or squat at a low desk. Schoolboys would sit cross-legged for lessons.

Gaining a good education

Boys who did go to school started at about five years old. Students learned **hieratic** script first, and practiced by writing sayings and stories on wooden boards or on pieces of broken pot and stone chips, called **ostraca**. Teachers were strict, and students who misbehaved were beaten. As boys grew older and mastered hieratic, they began studying **hieroglyphs**. Older boys were also taught mathematics, while some studied **astronomy**, geography, history, or law. By their teens, boys were ready to leave school and start work.

Perfect papyrus

Papyrus paper was one of the Egyptians' most useful inventions. It was made from the tall papyrus reeds that grow on the banks of the Nile River. The reeds were peeled and soaked, then sliced into strips. The strips were beaten flat and laid on top of one another in a criss-cross pattern to form a square sheet. Next, the sheet was pressed under a heavy weight, while the strips dried and stuck together. The final stage was to glue several sheets together to make a scroll.

Writing cases

This hieroglyphic sign shows a scribe's basic writing equipment. The upside-down U represents a strap, which went over the scribe's shoulder. From it hangs a wooden palette, with two round holes for holding solid cakes of black and red ink. At the other end of the strap are a pot for the water the scribe used to wet his inks and a container for his reed pens. The hieroglyph represents the sound "sesh," and when followed by the sign for a man, it meant "scribe."

MUMMIES AND THE AFTERLIFE

Archaeologists collect clues about the past from the bodies and possessions people left behind, as well as from written evidence. The ancient Egyptians left a wealth of **artifacts** behind, including hundreds of preserved bodies called **mummies**. Mummification is a process in which a dead body is dried out to stop it from decaying. The Egyptians practiced mummification because they believed in a life after death in which people still needed their bodies and possessions.

Mummifying a body properly was a long and costly process, so it was mainly practiced by the wealthy. Afterward, mummies were placed in **tombs**, with all the objects they would need in the **Afterlife**. The most splendid burials were given to the rulers of Egypt, the **pharaohs**.

▽ *One of the mummies found at Deir el-Bahri was that of Pharaoh Seti I (reigned 1294–1279 B.C.E.). It is one of the best preserved of all the pharaoh mummies that have been discovered so far.*

The royal tomb at Deir el-Bahri

It was not until the 1870s that any royal mummies were discovered. Then, a family of Egyptian tomb-robbers stumbled across a hidden rock shaft at Deir el-Bahri, near the Valley of the Kings. Inside was a narrow passageway littered with piles of dusty wooden **coffins** and hundreds of precious **burial goods**, including **papyri** and funeral figurines.

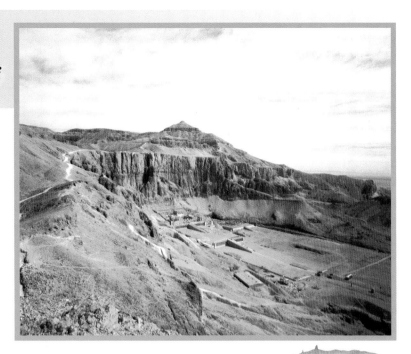

▷ *The rock shaft leading to the tomb of Seti I was found in the cliffs not far from the temple at Deir el-Bahri on the west bank of the Nile River.*

For ten years the tomb-robbers kept their discovery secret, stealing the burial goods and selling them to **antiquities** dealers. But so many precious things appeared on the market that the Egyptian Antiquities Service decided to investigate where they were coming from. The tomb-robbers were tracked down, arrested, and forced to lead German Egyptologist Emile Brugsch (1842–1930) to their hoard. To his amazement, when he read the names on the coffins, Brugsch realized that they contained many of the greatest rulers in Egyptian history. More than 50 pharaohs, queens, **courtiers**, and other royals were buried there. This was one of the most important finds in the history of **Egyptology**.

EYEWITNESS

"I made the best examination of them [the coffins] I could by the light of my torch, and at once saw that they contained the mummies of royal personages of both sexes."

(Emile Brugsch, describing his discovery at Deir el-Bahri on July 6, 1881)

Archaeology Challenge

Although **archaeological** treasures are still sometimes found by accident, archaeologists today have a range of sophisticated equipment to help them hunt below ground. Radar is short for RAdio Direction And Ranging. It detects the position of objects by sending out radio signals towards them and interpreting the way the signals are bounced back. Developed in the 1930s, radar was not used on archaeological sites until the early 1990s. It has proved particularly useful in finding underground hollows, such as tunnels and tombs.

Making a mummy

No ancient Egyptian description of the mummification process has been found, but we do have an eyewitness account from the Greek traveler and historian Herodotus (c. 485–425 B.C.E.), who visited Egypt in about 450 B.C.E. Modern scientific analysis of **mummies** has proved that his description was fairly accurate.

△ *Mummification was carried out by special priests who sometimes wore head masks to show that they represented the jackal-headed god Anubis, guardian of the dead.*

The process took 70 days and began with washing and cleansing the body. The brain was pulled out through the nose with a hook and thrown away. Then a slit was cut in the left side of the body and the intestines, liver, lungs, and stomach were removed. These four organs were preserved separately and later placed in special **canopic jars**. The heart was left in the body.

The next stage involved covering the body in a natural salt, called natron, which dried the body out and killed the bacteria that cause decay. After about 40 days, the natron was washed off and the body was stuffed with linen or sawdust. The skin was massaged with ointments to make it supple, and the body was coated in resin to make it waterproof.

Canopic jars

Canopic jars held a dead person's mummified organs. The jars were often sealed with stoppers shaped like the heads of the four sons of Horus, one of the chief Egyptian gods. The Egyptians believed that this would place the organs under the gods' protection. Ape-headed Hapy (left) looked after the lungs. Hawk-headed Qebehsenuef looked after the intestines. Dog-headed Duamutef protected the stomach, and human-headed Imsety the liver.

Archaeology Challenge

In the past, mummies were often damaged when they were unwrapped by people interested in how they were preserved. Modern scientific techniques allow archaeologists to study mummies without damaging them. Sometimes a computerized piece of hospital equipment, called a CAT scan, is used. This machine takes a series of X-rays of the body, then puts them together to produce a 3-D image that can be viewed from all angles.

△ *A mummy inside its painted wooden coffin is about to enter a CAT scan machine.*

The body was then wrapped from head to foot with linen bandages. The last layer was a shroud—a large piece of linen wrapped around the entire body. The mummy's face was covered with a mask that showed a portrait of the dead person. Finally, the mummy was laid inside a **coffin**, or sometimes a series of coffins, one inside the other. It was now ready for the funeral.

Cosy coffin

Coffins were often made of wood, which was then plastered and decorated. The face on the lid was an idealized portrait of the dead person.

This coffin belonged to a priestess who died about 3,000 years ago. The lower half is decorated with paintings of gods and prayers to protect the priestess on her journey to the **Afterlife.**

When nobles and royalty were buried, their wooden coffins were placed inside a large stone coffin, called a **sarcophagus.**

THE PYRAMID BUILDERS

The **mummies** of Egyptian **pharaohs** were placed in special **tombs** designed to keep them safe throughout the **Afterlife**. The largest and most famous of these tombs are the pyramids, but unfortunately they were not as safe as their builders hoped. Tomb-robbing was practiced from ancient times onward. Archaeologists have now excavated more than 100 pyramids, but found that all of them had been broken into by tomb-robbers. None of the pyramids contained any pharaoh mummies.

The Great Pyramid at Giza

The pyramids were a magnificent feat of **engineering**. They were built thousands of years ago, and yet many of them still stand today, towering above the desert sand. The largest is the Great Pyramid at Giza, west of the modern-day Egyptian capital, Cairo.

▽ *This is what the Great Pyramid at Giza looks like today, more than 4,500 years after it was built. When new, the whole structure was topped with a triangular capstone and encased in huge slabs of polished white limestone which gleamed and glistened in the sunlight.*

▷ *Inside the Great Pyramid are three chambers, linked by passageways. The pharaoh's empty* **sarcophagus** *was found in the King's chamber and remains there today. The two other burial chambers were never completed or used.*

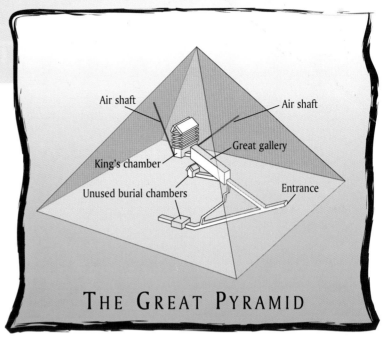

Air shaft
Air shaft
Great gallery
King's chamber
Entrance
Unused burial chambers

THE GREAT PYRAMID

This pyramid was the tomb of the pharaoh Khufu (reigned 2569–2566 B.C.E.). It was 481 feet (147 meters) high when finished. Work began in the mid-2500s B.C.E. and took 20 years to build. A staggering 2.5 million blocks of limestone went into the pyramid, each weighing around 2.5 tons!

Centuries of secrets

Egyptologists have been attempting to uncover the secrets of the pyramids ever since the first detailed **surveys** by experts traveling with Napoleon's army became public. Archaeologists have explored and mapped the pyramids inside and out, yet the discoveries continue. In 1993, for instance, archaeologists sent a robot camera into a narrow shaft leading up from one of the two unused burial chambers in the Great Pyramid. To their amazement, the robot photographed a stone door with two copper handles. For nine years people wondered what lay behind the door—hidden treasures, perhaps? Then, in 2002, another robot was sent up the shaft to drill a hole through the door and photograph what lay beyond.

Sadly, the robot's view was blocked by a wall, so we will have to wait a little longer to uncover the shaft's secrets!

Fantasy or Fact?

At just eight inches (twenty centimeters) square, the two shafts rising from the King's chamber in the Great Pyramid at Giza are extremely narrow. For many years archaeologists thought they were just air shafts. But recent research shows that when the pyramid was completed, the two shafts were in line with two stars—Sirius and Thuban in the constellation of Draco. Many people now think the shafts were designed to guide the dead pharaoh's soul up to the Afterlife.

DID YOU KNOW? In 1837, a cartouche found in the Great Pyramid identified Khufu as its builder.

Pyramid designers and builders

The architects

The first pyramid was designed by Imhotep, for the **pharaoh** Djoser (reigned 2667–2648 B.C.E.). It was built at Saqqara, south of Giza, and when it was completed in about 2650 B.C.E., it had a rectangular base and stepped sides. The true pyramid, with a square base and smooth-sloping sides, developed during the reign of Sneferu (reigned 2613–2589 B.C.E.). Sneferu was the father of Khufu, for whom the Great Pyramid at Giza was built.

WHO WAS Imhotep?

Imhotep's **tomb** has not yet been discovered, and we do not know when he was born or when he died. **Inscriptions** have told us that he was the architect who designed the first pyramid, at Saqqara, around 4,650 years ago. We also know that he was the pharaoh Djoser's **vizier**. The Egyptians respected Imhotep greatly, and in later centuries they began to worship him as a god of wisdom, writing, and medicine.

▽ *Some archaeologists think that the pyramid builders made ramps, up which they could haul the blocks of stone.*

Ramps

Workers and construction methods

People once believed that the pyramids were built by slaves, but archaeologists now think that hundreds of skilled stonemasons were employed to cut the stone and the unskilled labor was carried out by thousands of peasant farmers. Each year the Nile River flooded, covering the fields for about three months—farmers only had to work on the pyramids during this flood season.

No descriptions of pyramid-building have been found, so archaeologists do not know what methods were used. They are fairly certain that ramps were made so that the huge stone

Moving mountains

Another puzzle is how the Egyptians pulled the pyramid blocks up the construction ramp. The most likely answer is based on paintings like this. It shows a load of blocks being transported on a large wooden sledge, hauled by a team of men. Using a sledge would reduce the load to as little as one-tenth of its weight.

blocks could be hauled up. The ramps would have grown higher as the pyramid grew larger, but no one knows what shape they were. Some people think a single ramp was built at the front of the pyramid, while others believe the ramp spiraled up around it. Unless future **excavations** uncover new evidence, the pyramid-builders' techniques will remain a mystery.

River transportation

Although we are not certain how pyramid blocks were moved on land, we do know they were floated on boats from the quarries to the pyramid site. The Nile River runs through the heart of Egypt, and boats were the main form of transportation. Most were similar in shape to these model boats, which came from a tomb. Small boats were made from bundles of **papyrus** reeds. They were used for local travel and for fishing or hunting. Larger, wooden boats were used in war or to transport heavy loads long distances.

DID YOU KNOW? The true pyramid shape may have been meant to represent the Sun's spreading rays.

PHARAOHS AND GOVERNMENT

About 1,000 years after they were first built, pyramids began to go out of fashion. They were meant to keep the **pharaohs** and their possessions safe for eternity. Though no matter how many hidden entrances and false passages pyramids contained, they were still looted by tomb-robbers. The pharaoh Thutmose I (reigned 1504–1492 B.C.E.) asked his architect Ineni to come up with a new, safer kind of **tomb**.

The Valley of the Kings

From then on, the **mummies** of Egypt's rulers were hidden away in rock tombs carved out of the sides of a remote valley in the desert mountains of Upper Egypt. Today the site is known as the Valley of the Kings. As far as safety went, however, the new rock-cut tombs were little improvement on the pyramids. When Egyptologists began excavating in the Valley in the 1800s, every tomb they came across was found to have been broken into during ancient times.

The forgotten tomb of Tutankhamen

Only one archaeological team was allowed to work in the Valley at a time, and in 1915 the permit passed to Howard Carter. By then, most archaeologists believed that no more tombs remained to be discovered, but Carter believed that at least one was still hidden.

VALLEY OF THE KINGS

Rameses VII

To the Nile Valley

Rameses IV

Rameses III
Yuya & Thuya
Rameses XI

Merneptah   Rameses II
Tutankhamen   Rameses IX
Rameses VI

Amenhotep II

Amenmese
Mei-her-peri   Rameses I
Tawsert   Sethos I   Hatshepsut
Rameses X

Thutmose I   Mentuherkhopshet
Seti II   Thutmose IV

0   100 m
0   100 yards   N

Thutmose III

△ One of the world's most famous burial grounds, the Valley of the Kings is on the west bank of the Nile River, opposite the modern-day town of Luxor. More than 60 tombs have been found there, made up of passageways and chambers cut out of the limestone cliffs that surround the Valley.

WHO WAS Howard Carter?

Howard Carter (1874–1939) was just seventeen when he arrived in Egypt. His first job was as an artist, copying tomb paintings. Later he trained as an excavator, and in 1899 he was given a senior position in the Egyptian **Antiquities** Service. He resigned in 1903, and worked as an artist and antiquities dealer until 1908, when financial support from Lord Carnarvon allowed him to return to **excavation.** Following his discovery of Tutankhamen's tomb in 1922, Carter spent the remaining seventeen years of his life recording and analyzing his finds.

Little was known then about the pharaoh Tutankhamen (reigned 1336–1327 B.C.E.), but Carter hoped to change this. His search was funded by his sponsor, Lord Carnarvon (1866–1923), who was a wealthy amateur Egyptologist. The hunt took years, but on November 4, 1922, Carter's workers found a sunken staircase. At the bottom they uncovered the top of a blocked doorway that was coated in plaster and stamped with official **seals.** It seemed to be the entrance to a tomb. Carter sent a telegram to his sponsor, who was in England, and ordered his men to refill the staircase until Lord Carnarvon could join them.

▽ *This photograph shows the mysterious doorway found by Carter's team in November 1922. Further excavation uncovered sixteen steps leading down to it.*

EYEWITNESS

"At last have made wonderful discovery in Valley; a magnificent tomb with seals intact; recovered same for your arrival; congratulations."

(Howard Carter's 1922 telegram to Lord Carnarvon in England)

Tutankhamen's treasures

The tension mounts

Lord Carnarvon hurried to Egypt, and on November 24, 1922, **excavation** work began again. This time the whole doorway was uncovered. Stamped into the plaster at the bottom of the door was a **seal** bearing one of Tutankhamen's royal titles. Carter and Carnarvon now knew they had found the **pharaoh's tomb**, but would they find anything left inside?

A long passageway full of rubble lay beyond the tomb entrance. As Carter's workers cleared it, they found evidence of a robbers' tunnel dug in ancient times. On November 26, the excavators stood at the end of the emptied passageway, in front of a second doorway. Carter made a small hole in it and peered inside. To his amazement the chamber beyond was crammed with goods.

△ *This was the sight that met Carter's eyes when he peered into the first chamber of Tutankhamen's tomb. In the center of the photograph is a couch with legs shaped like an animal's body.*

The tomb had four chambers. Robbers had managed to break into one of them, but they had taken little. It seemed as though they had been caught and stopped. Hundreds of Tutankhamen's possessions remained inside. Even his **mummy** was still there, safe inside a stone **sarcophagus** and three richly decorated **coffins**.

WHO WAS Tutankhamen?

Tutankhamen's name is very well known today, but little is known about his life. No one is certain who his parents were. He became pharaoh in 1336 B.C.E., after the death of the pharaoh Akhenaten. Therefore it is likely that Tutankhamen was Akhenaten's younger brother or son. Tutankhamen was only eight or nine years old when he was crowned. Less than ten years later, in 1327 B.C.E., he died and was buried in the Valley of the Kings.

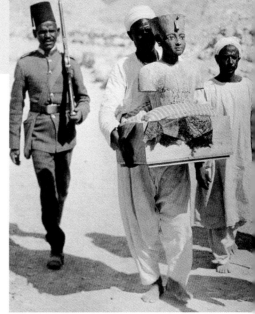

▷ *Egyptian workers helped to excavate and clear Tutankhamen's tomb. The original position of each artifact was carefully recorded before it was removed for painstaking study, cleaning, and preservation. Larger objects had to be taken apart and put back together once outside the tomb.*

Fantasy or Fact?

A mystery surrounding Tutankhamen is how he died. Two major autopsies were carried out on his mummified body. The first, in 1925, revealed his height (about 5 feet 4 inches; 1.63 meters) and his age at death (17 to 19 years old). By the time of the second autopsy in 1968, X-rays were available. The X-rays showed that Tutankhamen's skull had been damaged, suggesting that he was killed by an accidental or deliberate blow to the head. We may never know for certain, but some archaeologists now believe that Tutankhamen's short reign was brought to an end by murder.

Every object tells a story

It took Carter's team years to empty the tomb. Chairs, beds, chariots, weapons, musical instruments, and games had been buried with the pharaoh, along with clothes, cosmetics, and jewelry. There were also baskets of food, and a wreath of flowers that had been placed inside one of the coffins. Tutankhamen's tomb turned out to be the richest find in the history of **archaeology**, jam-packed with objects that give us a rare and vivid picture of upper-class life in ancient Egyptian times.

Finding out about the pharaoh

Egyptian society

Written and visual evidence tells us that the ancient Egyptians worshiped their ruler, the **pharaoh,** as the living son of a god. They were so in awe of him that even nobles would kiss the ground below his feet. Everyone and everything in Egypt belonged to the pharaoh, and he was head of the government, the priesthood, the army, and the law courts.

The **vizier** led the government and, after the pharaoh, was the most important person in Egypt. Then came the high priests, who were responsible for all aspects of religion and worship, followed by the commanders-in-chief of the army and navy. Egypt was divided into 42 districts, called nomes, and each nome had its own governor, who reported to the vizier.

Below these top officials were thousands of **scribes** who carried out day-to-day business, such as collecting taxes and maintaining law and order. The Egyptians did not use money, so taxes were paid in goods, such as grain and animals. Below the scribes were artists and other skilled craftspeople, and right at the bottom were all the hard-working farmers, who provided the food that kept everyone in Egypt alive.

Royal symbols

The head of Tutankhamen's **mummy** was protected by this solid gold death mask. It portrays him in his everyday crown, called the *nemes.* In real life, no type of Egyptian crown seems to have been made of solid gold. The *nemes* was actually made of striped cloth. Tutankhamen's mask shows another symbol of the pharaoh's power—the false beard, which in real life was made of wood and tied on with a strap.

Seat of power

Another of the treasures in Tutankhamen's **tomb** was a magnificent throne, made of wood coated in sheets of gold and silver. The back panel (left) shows Tutankhamen with his wife, Ankhesenamen. Gold was a holy material for the ancient Egyptians. They believed that the gods' bodies were made of gold, and they also associated gold with the Sun and everlasting life.

War and weapons

Only a few pharaohs actually took part in battles, but the pharaoh was always head of the army. Therefore pharaohs were often portrayed fighting, to symbolize their bravery—as in the painting on this box found in Tutankhamen's tomb. Egyptian armies were made up of foot soldiers, who fought with spears, swords, and daggers; and charioteers armed with bows and arrows. In real life, a chariot would have held two men— a driver and an archer.

TEMPLES AND GODS

The Egyptians worshiped hundreds of gods and goddesses. **Temples** were believed to be their earthly homes. It was every **pharaoh's** duty to build temples and to make sure that offerings were made to keep the gods happy. In return, the gods would bless the people with everything from good health and harvests to victory in battle. Like the pyramids, Egyptian temples were built from stone and have lasted through the ages. More temples have survived than any other kind of building.

The great temple complex at Karnak

Egypt's largest and most important holy site was at Karnak, near the modern-day town of Luxor. The temples and other buildings that can be seen there today were begun about 3,500 years ago. Beneath the ground, archaeologists have found traces of earlier structures dating back another 1,500 years. Nearly every pharaoh added to Karnak, often tearing down earlier structures and reusing the stone to build new ones.

▽ *The tall stone pillars with the pyramid-shaped tops in this part of the Temple of Amun at Karnak are called obelisks. Egyptian rulers often had obelisks put up in front of temples, but many were removed from Egypt during the 1800s, including the "Cleopatra's Needle" obelisks now in London and New York.*

◁ *A series of massive gateways lead into the Temple of Amun, each built by a different pharaoh. Beyond the first gateway is a courtyard, beyond the second is the* **hypostyle hall**, *and deep in the heart of the temple is the* **shrine** *where, people believed, the god's spirit lived in his statue. These enormous carved and painted columns once held up the stone roof of the hypostyle hall.*

When European travelers arrived in Egypt in the 1800s, little was left of the temples' ancient glory. Great chunks of roof, walls, and columns had collapsed, while the parts of the buildings that remained standing were largely buried in sand. Over the past hundred or so years, archaeologists have started on the vast task of **excavation** and **restoration**. The main temples have been excavated, but buried deep beneath them lies unexplored evidence which will keep archaeologists busy for many generations to come.

EYEWITNESS

"I seemed alone in the midst of all that is most sacred . . .; a forest of enormous columns, adorned all around with beautiful figures, and various ornaments . . ."

(Italian excavator Giovanni Belzoni, on entering the hypostyle hall in the Temple of Amun, 1816)

Archaeology Challenge

Sometimes **archaeology** is not only about excavating sites, but about rescuing them. In the 1960s, a dam was built across the Nile River, south of Aswan. The region's temples were in danger of vanishing underwater once the river rose behind the completed dam. An international appeal was launched for money to save the most important temples. It was possible then to take the temples apart and rebuild them on new sites. The largest building to be moved in this way was the great temple carved into the rock cliffs of Abu Simbel. It is fronted by 66-foot- (20-meter-) high statues of its builder, the pharaoh Rameses II (reigned 1279–1213 B.C.E.).

Priests and worshipers

Archaeologists have created an image of how the
Egyptians worshiped, both by studying
papyrus scrolls containing hymns,
prayers, and official documents,
such as records of **temple** offerings,
and by looking at carvings and
paintings on temple and **tomb** walls.
Only the **pharaoh** and a few leading priests could
approach the holiest part of the temple, called the **sanctuary**. Here was the
shrine, where people believed the god's spirit lived in its statue. Ordinary
people were sometimes allowed in the temple courtyard.

EYEWITNESS

"My Lord is my defender, I know
his strength,

He helps with a strong arm and a
compassionate look.

He alone is the powerful one."

(Prayer to Amun, 12th century B.C.E.)

Galaxy of gods

The tall feather-plumed headdress tells us that the
statue on the left is of Amun, the king of the
Egyptian gods. Amun was usually portrayed
in human form, although other gods were
often shown as animals or with animal
heads. Only the most important gods had
their own temples and priests. Most of
the major gods represented forces such as
the Sun or the Nile River, or were linked with
important events in life, such as birth or death.

▷ *Taweret, goddess of birth and protector
of women and children, had a hippo's head
and body. She was also shown with a
lion's paws and a crocodile's tail.*

The gods' servants

The Egyptians called their priests "servants of the god." They were mostly men, although until about 1600 B.C.E. it was common for noblewomen to serve as priestesses of the goddess of love, Hathor.

Priests did not hold public services and few worked at the temple all year round. Instead there was a rotating system, with different groups spending one month at the temple doing their priestly duties, followed by three months at home doing their usual jobs. Most of a priest's duties had to do with the everyday organization of the temple complex—running libraries, workshops, storerooms, and so on. Only a few special priests were allowed to serve the god by taking part in temple **rituals**.

Holy service

The most important temple rituals were all about caring for the statue in which the god's spirit was believed to live. Every day at dawn, a special priest would burn **incense** to **purify** the air, and pour an offering of clean water in front of the god's shrine. The god's statue was then taken out, undressed, and washed, before being clothed in clean linen and covered with fresh make-up. Real food was served for the god's breakfast and at similar rituals later in the day.

▷ *Thoth, god of wisdom and patron god of scribes, was shown as a baboon, an ibis bird, or an ibis-headed man.*

Magic and medicine

In ancient Egypt magic was central in everything, from temple rituals to medical treatment. Magical charms called amulets were worn to bring people luck and protect them from harm. Amulets came in many shapes, but the scarab beetle was one of the most popular. Although doctors were skilled at setting bones and making herbal remedies, people believed that the most effective cures were brought about by a combination of magic and medicine.

EVERYDAY LIFE OF THE WEALTHY

Pharaohs and their families were not the only Egyptians to be buried in rock-cut **tombs**. Nobles and wealthy government officials also commissioned craftspeople to create splendid tombs to house their mummified bodies throughout eternity. Tombs with wall-carvings or paintings are known as decorated tombs, and as many as 400 of them have been found in and around the Valley of the Kings.

△ *Nebamun is shown here hunting river birds. He has brought his wife (standing behind him) and daughter (sitting) along for the outing. He is standing on a small papyrus-reed boat and, in one hand, is holding a snake-shaped throwing stick, which was hurled at prey to stun or kill it.*

The tomb of Nebamun

Some of the finest wall-paintings are from the tomb of an official named Nebamun, who lived in the 1300s B.C.E. The paintings show him and his family hunting, feasting, and generally having a good time in the **Afterlife**. They can still be seen today, but not in Egypt. The paintings are in the British Museum in London, which obtained them in 1821. The paintings are from a tomb at Thebes, discovered by British official Henry Salt, but the exact location of the tomb is now lost. The tomb was probably robbed by ancient Egyptian tomb-robbers soon after Nebamun was buried, and was empty when Henry Salt removed some of the wall-paintings.

EYEWITNESS

"Our attention was principally drawn by the paintings decorating the four walls and ceiling . . . preserved as fresh and intact as the day . . . they were first made."

(Spanish Consul-General Eduardo Toda y Güell, on entering the tomb of court official Sennedjem [1200s B.C.E.] on February 1, 1886)

Magical mirror of life

The Egyptians believed that the images in decorated tombs could magically supply a dead person's needs in the Afterlife. For instance, if a painting showed a noble hunting, then he would be able to enjoy this pastime in the Afterlife.

Archaeology Challenge

The decorated tombs in the Valley of the Kings are under threat, especially from the thousands of tourists who walk through them everyday. Moisture from their breath and body sweat harms the paintings, as do the electric lights that are needed to guide people through the darkness underground. Many of the finest tombs have now been closed in order to protect them. But tourists will still be able to see their marvelous paintings. A project is underway to make replica tombs, using the latest laser-scanning and computer technology to create completely accurate "virtual reality" copies.

The artists themselves are rarely shown, and there is little evidence of how they worked. Archaeologists believe that a sketch was made first on a small board marked with a squared grid. A full-size grid was marked on the tomb wall, and the sketch was scaled up and copied onto it. The final stage was to paint in all the color detail.

◁ *Archaeologists think that using a grid helped artists keep figures and objects in their paintings in proportion. For example, they could ensure that each lower arm was four squares of the grid long. People were nearly always shown with their eyes, chest, and shoulders facing forward.*

Pastimes

The thrill of the chase

Like Nebamun, wealthy Egyptians enjoyed hunting and fishing, often going after much bigger prey than birds. Hippotamuses and crocodiles lived in the Nile River in ancient times, while lions, ostriches, and wild bulls roamed across the desert. Some **tomb** paintings show hunters facing death, trying to spear fierce river creatures. Others show them in their chariots chasing after wild desert animals.

Perfect party

Another of the beautiful paintings from Nebamun's tomb shows a banquet in full swing. Seated guests are waited on by servants. The women have longer hair than the men, and some men have shaved heads. Nearly everyone has a cone of perfumed ointment on their head. As the cones slowly melted from body heat, they kept people cool and smelling sweet.

Getting in the party spirit

When not out hunting, the wealthy loved to party. Guests at a banquet would wear their finest clothes and jewelry, and be served beer, wine, and a range of tasty dishes. Food left in tombs and shown in paintings tells us that the wealthy dined on a wide selection of farmed meats, including beef, lamb, and goat, and wild game, such as antelope and gazelle. They also ate a variety of vegetables and fruit, as well as bread and honey-sweetened cakes and pastries. Dishes were flavored with herbs, such as mint and thyme, and spices, such as cumin and coriander.

Music to the ears

The paintings in Nebamun's tomb show that musicians and dancers provided entertainment for the guests at the banquet. Musicians often supplied a background beat by clapping their hands, as the three women to the left of the flute-player are doing in this wall painting. Many musical instruments have been found in Egyptian tombs, including harps, lutes, flutes, and tambourines, but we have no idea what Egyptian music sounded like—they never wrote down the tunes.

▷ *This ancient Egyptian harp dates from between 1200 and 500 B.C.E.*

Child's play

Children played with simple, homemade toys in ancient Egyptian times, including cloth or leather balls, and model animals carved from wood. Some of their games are still played by children today, such as leapfrog and tug-of-war. Children from wealthy families had more playtime than the poor, who had to work in the fields alongside their fathers or help their mothers at home.

Fantasy or Fact?

This lengthy discussion of tombs may give the impression that the Egyptians were unhappy people who spent all their time thinking about death. But nothing could be further from the truth. Decorated tombs show us all the things the Egyptians enjoyed doing while they were alive, and that they loved life so much that they wanted to carry on experiencing the same activities throughout eternity!

Fashion

Cool clothing

Egypt is a hot country and clothing was designed to keep people cool. Rich and poor people wore similar clothes, although the wealthy could afford better quality fabric. The basic outfit for men was a kilt-like skirt, and for women, a long, sheath-like dress. The only underwear for both sexes was a **loincloth**, and most people wore sandals made from palm leaves or **papyrus**. By about the 1500s B.C.E., wealthy men also sometimes wore a T-shaped tunic, while women wrapped a large pleated shawl around their body, tying it under their breasts. Young children went naked, and older ones dressed like their parents.

△ *This painting from the tomb of a wealthy court official, Sennedjem, at Deir el-Medina shows pleated clothing.*

Luxury linen

The clothes of most Egyptians, rich and poor, were made from linen, which was woven from the flax plant. Only the wealthy could afford the finest, whitest fabric. By the 1300s B.C.E., fashionable women were wearing linen so fine that it was see-through. Wall-paintings and carvings show that it became stylish to wear heavily pleated clothes, but archaeologists are not sure how the pleating was done. In one **tomb** they found this grooved wooden board that may have been used to press pleats into clothing.

Finishing touches

Wealthy men and women also had elaborate hairstyles, make-up, and jewelry. Hair was braided or curled, and on special occasions people wore wigs. Children often had their heads shaved, apart from a single lock on one side of the head.

Archaeologists have a wide range of evidence for Egyptian clothes and beauty products, from **artifacts** placed in tombs to the images in wall-paintings and carvings. In 1974, they even found the remains of a wig-maker's workshop at Deir el-Bahri.

▷ *This gold and turquoise collar belonged to the daughter of pharaoh Amenemhat II (reigned 1922–1878 B.C.E.).*

Glittering prizes

Egyptians loved jewelry. Men and women wore necklaces, bracelets, armlets, and anklets, as well as hair ornaments, rings, and earrings. The most valuable pieces were made from gold or silver, and set with semi-precious stones, such as lapis lazuli, turquoise, and carnelian. Most of the gold was mined in southern Egypt and Nubia, but silver was imported from a number of Mediterranean and west Asian countries. Valuable Egyptian goods, such as linen and papyrus, were exchanged in this kind of overseas trade.

Beautiful people

All sorts of cosmetics and beauty tools have been found in Egyptian tombs, from eye-paint and lip-paint to make-up bottles, mirrors, tweezers, razors, combs, and hair-curling tongs. Both men and women wore make-up. Chemical tests have shown that green eye-paint was made from ground malachite (a copper ore) and black from galena (a lead ore). Red ochre (a type of soil) was used to make lip gloss and rouge for the cheeks.

DID YOU KNOW? Wealthy people hung gold rings in their pet cats' ears and noses.

EVERYDAY LIFE OF THE WORKERS

Archaeologists have excavated only a small number of sites that tell us about ancient Egyptian houses. This is partly because, unlike the grand stone pyramids and **temples**, Egyptian homes were mostly built from bricks made from sun-baked river mud—and mud-bricks deteriorate far more quickly than stone. Another reason for the lack of evidence is that many modern-day villages have been built on and from the rubble of earlier ones. Then, as now, most homes were built in the narrow strips of fertile land along the Nile River.

△ At its largest, Deir el-Medina was made up of about 70 houses. The lower parts of the house walls (above) were built from stone, cemented with mud and plaster. The rest of the walls were made of mud bricks that were plastered and whitewashed. The homes of the wealthy, in the towns and countryside, were built in a similar way, but were much larger, with more rooms.

The workers' village of Deir el-Medina

Most of the ancient villages that have survived are close to the desert. They were built for the craftspeople who worked on the decorated **tombs** and the pyramids. One of the best-preserved is the village of Deir el-Medina. It housed the families of the men building the rock-cut tombs in the Valley of the Kings. Although **artifacts** were found at the site in the early 1800s, the chief **excavation** work was carried out from 1905 to 1909 by Italian Ernesto Schiaparelli (1856–1928), and between 1917 and 1947 by Frenchman Bernard Bruyère (1879–1971). As well as the remains of the craftspeople's homes, a vast amount of written evidence was discovered that gives a vivid picture of everyday work and home life.

Home sweet home

The excavations at Deir el-Medina revealed that the village had one central street, with houses on both sides separated by a few side alleys. The houses were narrow and had roughly the same layout. Generally, each was made up of four small rooms, one behind the other. The front room, used by the women, seems to have been a reception area for visitors. Behind was a living room, used by the men, which was probably also used for sleeping. People may also have slept on the roof. The third room was used for storage, while the final room was where the women cooked the family meals.

▽ *This cross-section shows the plan of a typical house at Deir el-Medina, with four rooms and a staircase leading to the roof. Cellars beneath the house provided cool storage places for jars of food and drink.*

Stairs

Kitchen

Storage

Cellar

Cellar

Reception area

Living room

DID YOU KNOW? The Deir el-Medina workers went on the first recorded strike in the 1200s B.C.E.

37

People at work

The village workers

The written evidence excavated at Deir el-Medina includes **papyri** and thousands of **ostraca**—chips of stone or pottery that **scribes** used like notepads. As well as records of the worker's tools, hours of work, and wages, there are letters, poems, and even laundry lists.

The people who worked on the **tombs** were stonemasons, carpenters, sculptors, and painters. Their work "week" was eight days long, followed by two days rest. Further down the social scale were the men who helped supply the craftspeople's daily needs for food, water, and so on. They included fishermen, gardeners, laundrymen, watercarriers, and woodcutters.

Working families

Women were thought to be less important than men in ancient Egypt. They are rarely shown working as anything other than servants, as in this wooden model, or as musicians and dancers. Written evidence shows that some women also worked as bakers, weavers, gardeners, and farmers. Most ordinary women spent their days cooking and cleaning. Girls helped their mothers, while boys worked alongside their fathers, learning their trade.

Tools of the trade

These wooden mallets and bronze chisels are stonemason tools found at Deir el-Medina. The chisels would have been used for shaping blocks of stone. Finer-pointed chisels with wooden handles would have been used for detailed work such as carving **hieroglyphs.**

The models of Meketra

In addition to the Deir el-Medina findings, archaeologists have collected a wealth of written and visual evidence from other sites throughout Egypt. The most vivid comes from beautifully detailed, painted wooden models that were placed in tombs to provide servants for the **Afterlife**. One of the finest collections of tomb models was found near Deir el-Bahri in 1920, in the tomb of Meketra, a powerful government official who died around 2000 B.C.E. The models, which formed a model estate, include a fascinating range of boats, as well as a brewery and bakery, a butcher's shop, a granary, and a carpenter's and a weaver's workshops.

EYEWITNESS

"The beam [lit up] a little world of 4,000 years ago, and I was gazing down into . . . a myriad of brightly painted little men going this way and that . . . "

(American archaeologist H. E. Winlock [1884–1950], on his first sight of the models of Meketra in 1920)

Carpenters at work

This exquisite 10-inch- (26-centimeter-) high model of a carpenter's workshop is one of the treasures from Meketra's tomb. It shows the workshop bustling with activity, as men cut planks, drill and chisel holes, and plane down and smooth surfaces. Apart from palm trees, few trees grew in Egypt. So, the best-quality wood was imported from abroad. This made wooden objects, such as furniture, expensive. Usually, the results of a carpenter's hard work were for his wealthy employer, not for his own home.

DID YOU KNOW? Clothes were washed in the Nile, where laundrymen had to watch out for crocodiles! **39**

Farming and food

Farmers and landowners

As paid professionals, carpenters and other craftspeople were fairly well-off. The poorest Egyptians were the farmers. Most farming land in Egypt was owned by the **pharaoh**, his nobles, or the **temples**. Farmers not only had to grow enough food to keep themselves and their families alive, but also had to pay a part of their grain harvest as a tax to the landowner. Tax-collecting **scribes** made regular visits to check that farmers got the best out of their land and did not cheat when declaring how much grain they had gathered at harvesttime.

Important crops

A farmer's chief grain crops were wheat and barley. These were turned into bread and beer, which made up the main diet of most Egyptians. Another important crop was flax, which was woven into cloth. A variety of vegetables were grown too, from onions, garlic, beans, and lentils, to cabbages, cucumbers, lettuces, and peas. Fruit crops included dates, figs, grapes, and melons. Although poor people rarely ate meat, farmers had eggs from their own ducks and chickens. Farmers looked after their landowner's herds of cattle, and used oxen to do heavy work like pulling the plow.

Harvesttime

This wall-painting of a harvest scene comes from the **tomb** of a wealthy scribe, named Menna, who died in about 1400 B.C.E.—and hoped to have a lot of grain in the **Afterlife!** The farmer on the left is cutting grain with a wooden sickle (a special harvesting blade), and the harvested corn is being carried away in a large basket.

Archaeology Challenge

Bread was the main food of most Egyptians, rich and poor, but chewing on it must have given them a terrible toothache. Dental examination of mummified Egyptian teeth shows that they were often worn down. Archaeologists discovered the cause of worn down teeth by analyzing loaves of bread that had been preserved for thousands of years in tombs. The ancient loaves of bread were full of stone grit. The grit came from the way grain was ground into flour—rubbing it between two stones.

Home brew

Beer was the favorite drink of ordinary Egyptians, but it was so thick and lumpy that it had to be sieved or sucked through a wooden strainer, which was like a straw. Beer was made at home by dissolving partially baked cakes of barley bread in water. This mixture was then strained and left to ferment into alcohol. Dates, honey, and spices were sometimes added to flavor the brew.

Water power

Crops will not grow without water, and because it hardly ever rains in Egypt, farmers rely on the Nile River. This lifting device is called a *shaduf,* and since ancient times people have used it to raise river water up on to farmland. Until it was dammed in the 1960s, the Nile flooded every year in June, covering the fields with rich mud and life-giving water. Farmers plowed their fields and sowed their crops after the floods went down in October or November.

ARCHAEOLOGY TODAY

The story of **Egyptology** is by no means over. Each year, more than 100 teams of Egyptian and foreign archaeologists are hard at work excavating and recording sites throughout Egypt. In other countries around the world, more teams of archaeologists are examining and conserving the **artifacts** held by their nations' museums. Some are continuing the long task of deciphering the **hieroglyphic** texts in Egypt and in museum collections. The objects found in the past 200 or so years will keep people busy for several hundred years to come!

Going over old ground

The modern-day emphasis on scientific **archaeology** means that **excavation** work is slower and more painstaking than it was in the early years of Egyptology. Much of it happens at sites that have already been excavated, where today's teams are searching for evidence that was missed the first time around.

A concern for modern Egyptologists is that many of the known sites are under threat. It is not just the **tombs** in the Valley of the Kings that are being harmed by exposure to tourists, but also monuments such as the Great Pyramid at Giza. Other ancient monuments are being damaged by weathering and by rising levels of underground water.

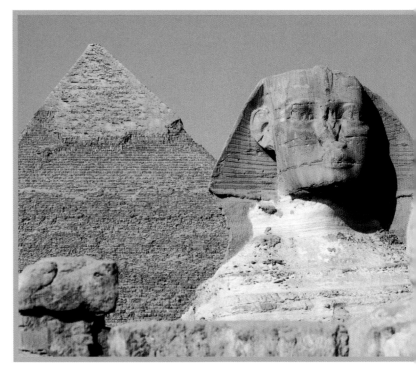

△ *You can clearly see how erosion by the weather has damaged the Great **Sphinx** at Giza.*

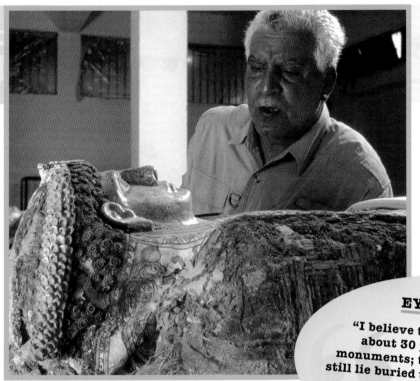

◁ Dr. Zahi Hawass examines a masked mummy, one of many found in 1996 at a cemetery discovered in the Bahariya Oasis, Egypt. It is estimated that the site could contain 10,000 mummies.

Searching for the new

The picture is not all discouraging, though, and exciting new discoveries continue to be made—even at well-known sites. In 1990, Director of the Giza Pyramids Excavation, Dr. Zahi Hawass (born 1947), made an extraordinary find at Giza, close to the Great Pyramid. He discovered a cemetery that turned out to contain more than 40 tombs belonging to the workers who built the pyramids more than 4,500 years ago. By studying the workers' bones, Hawass's team learned that the pyramid builders died relatively young—between the ages of 30 and 35. By contrast, government officials lived almost twice as long.

In 2002, a Swiss team literally stumbled across a previously unknown pyramid buried in the sand just a few miles to the south of Giza. It is not a large pyramid, and there was no **mummy** inside, but it is thought to have belonged to a **pharaoh's** wife, daughter, or sister. The story of Egyptology is still unfolding, and who knows what amazing finds may lie just around the corner!

TIMELINE OF ANCIENT EGYPT

There were three great ages in ancient Egyptian history: the Old, Middle, and New Kingdoms. Each age was followed by a period of unrest, **civil war**, and invasion. These periods are known as the Intermediate Periods.

The events in ancient Egyptian history took place so long ago that historians cannot be certain of the exact dates. You may discover that the dates given in this book are slightly different to those found in other sources.

About 5000 B.C.E.
The narrow strip of fertile land by the Nile River becomes known as Lower Egypt (the northern region) and Upper Egypt (the southern region).

About 3500 B.C.E.
Hieroglyphic writing develops.

About 3100 B.C.E.
Lower and Upper Egypt are united under one ruler named Menes.

2686–2181 B.C.E.
OLD KINGDOM

2650 B.C.E.
Egypt's first pyramid is built at Saqqara, for **Pharaoh** Djoser.

About 2580 B.C.E.
The Great Pyramid at Giza is completed for Pharaoh Khufu.

2181–2055 B.C.E.
First Intermediate Period
Civil war divides and weakens Egypt.

2055–1650 B.C.E.
MIDDLE KINGDOM

2055 B.C.E.
Upper and Lower Egypt are reunited by Mentuhotep II. He moves the capital from Memphis (in the north) to Thebes (in the south). He and his successors restore Egypt's wealth and power. Architecture, literature, and other arts flourish. The first great **temples** are built at Karnak.

1650–1550 B.C.E.
Second Intermediate Period
The Hyksos invade from Palestine and nearby, and conquer Lower Egypt.

1550–1069 B.C.E.
NEW KINGDOM

1550 B.C.E.
The Hyksos are driven out of Egypt and Ahmose I is crowned pharaoh. During the New Kingdom, Egypt becomes the strongest, wealthiest nation in the Middle East.

1504–1492 B.C.E.
Pharaoh Thutmose I reigns. He is the first Egyptian ruler to have a rock-cut **tomb** in the Valley of the Kings.

1352–1336 B.C.E.
Pharaoh Akhenaten rules Egypt. He forces his people to worship a single sun god, Aten.

1336–1327 B.C.E.
Tutankhamen is pharaoh. Egyptians may once again worship many gods.

1279–1213 B.C.E.
Rameses II (Rameses the Great) rules Egypt. The temple at Abu Simbel, beautiful additions to the temple complex at Karnak, and many other monuments are built during his reign.

1184–1153 B.C.E.
Rameses III reigns. Egypt is invaded by foreign armies from the north and its power begins to decline.

1069–747 B.C.E.
Third Intermediate Period
Civil war divides Egypt once more.

747–332 B.C.E.
LATE PERIOD

525–404 B.C.E.
Persia invades and takes control of Egypt. After the Persians are defeated, the country returns to Egyptian rule.

About 450 B.C.E.
The Greek traveler and historian Herodotus visits Egypt.

343–332 B.C.E.
Persia invades again, and regains control of Egypt.

332 B.C.E.–C.E. 395
GREEK-ROMAN PERIOD

332 B.C.E.
The Persians are overthrown by the armies of Alexander the Great. Egypt becomes part of the Greek Empire.

305–30 B.C.E.
After Alexander's death, the throne passes to one of his generals, Ptolemy. Ptolemy and his heirs rule Egypt.

196 B.C.E.
The Rosetta Stone is carved.

51–30 B.C.E.
Ptolemy's last heir, Cleopatra VII, rules. She ends her life when Egypt is conquered by the Romans and becomes part of the Roman Empire.

TIMELINE OF EGYPTOLOGY

1798–1801

The foundations of **Egyptology** are laid during the invasion of Egypt by French emperor Napoleon. His army is accompanied by a team of artists and scientists, who carry out the first detailed study of ancient Egyptian monuments. In 1799, one of Napoleon's soldiers finds the Rosetta Stone. This will be the key to understanding the hieroglyphic writing of the ancient Egyptians.

About 1800–1850

Foreign collectors flock to Egypt in search of **antiquities**. Many are adventurers who loot sites, causing the loss or damage of countless ancient **artifacts**. Others are scholars, such as German Egyptologist Karl Lepsius, who build on the work of the French expedition.

1822

French scholar Jean-François Champollion cracks the code of the Rosetta Stone and becomes the first person since ancient times to be able to read hieroglyphs.

1858

The plundering of ancient sites ends when French Egyptologist Auguste Mariette is put in charge of **excavation** in Egypt. Mariette founds the Egyptian Antiquities Service (now the Supreme Council for Antiquities) and the Egyptian Museum in Cairo.

1881

Frenchman Gaston Maspero succeeds Mariette as head of the Antiquities Service and the Egyptian Museum. A tomb containing **mummies** of more than 50 pharaohs, queens, **courtiers**, and other royals is excavated at Deir el-Bahri, near the Valley of the Kings.

1880s

The scientific recording, excavation, and **preservation** of archaeological sites is pioneered by the great British archaeologist Flinders Petrie.

1898

Serious excavation work begins in the Valley of the Kings. Many royal tombs are discovered, including that of one of Egypt's most powerful pharaohs, Thutmose III (reigned 1479–1425 B.C.E.).

1899

American archaeologist George Reisner begins excavations in Egypt, at Koptos near Luxor, setting similarly high standards to those of Petrie.

1903–1905

At the temple complex of Karnak, near Luxor, French Egyptologist Georges Legrain unearths the largest find of royal statues ever made in Egypt.

1905–09

Italian Egyptologist Ernesto Schiaparelli excavates the village of Deir el-Medina, uncovering the homes and tombs of workmen who built the royal tombs in the Valley of the Kings.

1920

At Deir el-Bahri, the tomb of the government official Meketra (died about 2000 B.C.E.) is excavated by American archaeologist Herbert Winlock. The discoveries include an amazing collection of wooden tomb models that illustrate many aspects of ancient Egyptian life.

1922

In the Valley of the Kings, British Egyptologist Howard Carter discovers the tomb of Pharaoh Tutankhamen (reigned 1336–1327 B.C.E.).

1954

At Giza, Egyptian archaeologist Kamal el-Mallakh makes an astounding discovery at the foot of the Great Pyramid of Pharaoh Khufu (reigned 2589–2566 B.C.E.)—a pit containing the pieces of the pharaoh's boat. When put back together, the boat is more than 141 feet (43 meters) long—the largest ancient Egyptian boat that has ever been discovered.

1960s

An international rescue effort saves more than twenty temples and other ancient holy sites from being flooded by the construction of a new dam to the south of Aswan, in Upper Egypt. The monuments are taken apart and rebuilt on higher ground.

1990

Egyptian archaeologist Dr. Zahi Hawass discovers the cemetery where the workers who built the Giza pyramids were buried.

1993

Archaeologists use a tiny robot camera to explore one of the shafts in the Great Pyramid at Giza.

1996

At the Bahariya Oasis in Egypt's Western Desert, a huge cemetery dating from the Greek-Roman Period (332 B.C.E.–C.E. 395) is discovered. It is believed to contain as many as 10,000 mummies.

2002

A few miles to the south of Giza, Swiss archaeologists find the ruins of a pyramid that was built more than 4,500 years ago. Around 110 pyramids have now been discovered in Egypt.

Afterlife
ancient Egyptians believed that a person's spirit, memory, and personality did not end with their death, but carried on to enjoy life in another world—the Afterlife

antiquity
object or building that has survived since ancient times

archaeology
scientific excavation and study of the remains of past societies, such as buildings, artwork, dead bodies, and tools, pottery, and other objects

artifact
object made by people, such as a tool or an ornament. Archaeologists often use the word "artifacts" to describe the objects they find that were made by people in past times.

astronomy
scientific study of the stars, planets, and other space bodies that make up the universe

autopsy
when doctors examine a dead body to find out how the person died

burial good
object buried with a dead body

canopic jar
one of four special jars used to store the intestines, liver, lungs, or stomach of a mummified body

cartouche
in Egyptian archaeology, a cartouche is an oval frame around the names of a god, a pharaoh, or a member of a pharaoh's family

civil war
war between people who belong to the same country or nation

coffin
box in which a dead person's body is buried

Coptic
language of the Copts, a people descended from the ancient Egyptians

courtier
person who attends a royal court

demotic
simplified form of ancient Egyptian hieroglyphs

dig (see **excavation**)

Egyptology
study of the language, customs, ideas, art, and history of ancient Egypt

engineering
use of scientific knowledge to design structures and machines, as well as tools, materials, and other products

excavation
process of excavating, that is digging up a building or area of land in order to look for ancient objects, ruins, or other evidence of the past

export
send or take goods to another country

famine
long-lasting shortage of food that causes widespread hunger and death

hieratic
flowing form of writing based on hieroglyphs

hieroglyphs
earliest form of Egyptian writing, in which pictures stand for sounds or words

hypostyle hall
temple hall with a roof held up by many columns

incense
substance that gives off a pleasing scent when burned

inscription
in archaeology, a historical or religious record that is carved, painted, or written on a hard surface such as stone or metal

loincloth
piece of cloth worn around the hips

medieval
relating to the Middle Ages, the period in European history between ancient and modern times (about C.E. 500 to 1500)

mummy
dead body that has been specially preserved to stop it from decaying. The process of doing this is called mummification.

ostracon (plural: ostraca)
flake of stone or piece of broken pottery used in ancient times for making rough notes and sketches

papyrus (plural: papyri)
tall river plant, and the name of a paper made from its reed-like stems. The ancient Egyptians used papyrus reeds to make everything from paper, baskets, and rope, to sandals, mats, and small boats.

pharaoh
title given by the ancient Egyptians to their kings. The word comes from the ancient Egyptian name for a royal palace—the "per-aa," or Great House.

pilgrim
person who makes a special journey to a holy site

prehistoric
time before writing was invented and history was recorded

preservation
saving something from being lost, damaged, or slowly crumbling or rotting away

purify
cleanse and make pure

radiocarbon dating
way of discovering the age of some objects by measuring the amount of a substance called carbon that they contain. It works because plants and animals absorb a special type of carbon, Carbon-14, from the air when they are alive. When they die, this carbon decays at a known rate. So, the amount present in a piece of wood, bone, or other material that was once part of a plant or animal reveals how old the material is.

restoration
when a building, painting, or other object is repaired or cleaned to return it to its former glory

ritual
special words and actions of a religious service or ceremony

sanctuary
holy place, such as a church or temple, as well as the holiest place inside it, such as the altar

sarcophagus
coffin carved from stone

scribe
person who could write; one of the officials or priests who carried out the everyday business of running ancient Egypt

scroll
roll of paper. In ancient Egypt, scrolls were made by joining several sheets of papyrus paper together.

seal
piece of clay stamped with signs, pictures, and writing. Seals were used to mark ownership, for example, seals stamped with a pharaoh's name showed that a tomb belonged to him.

shrine
sacred place, usually where people worship the body or statue of a god, saint, or other holy person

sphinx
in ancient legends, the sphinx was a monster with the body of a lion and the head of another creature, usually human. The ancient Egyptians carved many sphinx statues, large and small, but the most famous is the 66-foot- (20-meter-) high Great Sphinx that sits in front of the pyramids of Giza.

survey
detailed examination or investigation of a building or place, which often includes taking measurements so that an accurate record or map can be created

temple
building in which people worship, especially in ancient or non-Christian religions

tomb
special chamber, room, or hole specially cut into the ground, where a dead person's body is buried

vizier
person who ran a pharaoh's government, similar to a modern-day prime minister

FURTHER READING

Crosher, Judith. (Technology in the Time of) *Ancient Egypt*. Chicago: Raintree, 1998.

Devereux, Paul. *Archaeology: The Study of Our Past*. Milwaukee: Gareth Stevens, 2002.

Middleton, Hayden. *The Pyramids*. Chicago: Heinemann Library, 2003.

Moses, Brian. *An Egyptian Tomb*. Chicago: Raintree, 2001.

Orna-Ornstein, John. *Archaeology: Discovering the Past*. New York: Oxford University Press, 2002.

Pemberton, Delia. *Egyptian Mummies*. Chicago: Raintree, 2002.

Rees, Rosemary. *The Ancient Egyptians*. Chicago: Heinemann Library, 1997.

Williams, Brenda. *Ancient Egyptian Homes*. Chicago: Heinemann Library, 2003.